100 POEMS ON
POETS AND POETRY

100 POEMS ON
POETS AND POETRY

Lingaraj Rath

Translated by
Harekrushna Das

BLACK EAGLE BOOKS
Dublin, USA ● Bhubaneswar, Odisha

Black Eagle Books
USA address:
7464 Wisdom Lane
Dublin, OH 43016

India address:
E/312, Trident Galaxy, Kalinga Nagar,
Bhubaneswar-751003, Odisha, India

E-mail: info@blackeaglebooks.org
Website: www.blackeaglebooks.org

First International Edition Published by
Black Eagle Books, 2022

100 POEMS ON POETS AND POETRY
by **Lingaraj Rath**
Translated by **Harekrushna Das**

Original Copyright © Lingaraj Rath
Translation Copyright © Harekrushna Das

Cover & Interior Design: Ezy's Publication

ISBN- 978-1-64560-295-8 (Paperback)
Library of Congress Control Number: 2022942157

Printed in the United States of America

Dedicated to all Poets -
Past, Present & Future...

Words From The Poet

It is a well-known fact that the earliest literature of the world is written in verse. The treasure trove of knowledge, the Vedas, that are universally acknowledged to be Apaurusheya or unauthored, are also verse-literature. The predominance of poetry in human life can hardly be undermined. The noted spiritual writer and thinker, Manoj Das opines that the great literature written by Valmiki and Vyasa is the outcome of sheer inspiration. I, however, believe that the writings of all great poets also spring from the emotions and feelings that nestle in their hearts. I therefore began to develop a fascination about poets and their role in the society. And, the consequence of this zest is the present collection of poems on the singular theme of poets and poetry.

Conceived originally as mini-poems in Odia, a few have been published in the journal Rockpebbles in English rendition. Now, one hundred poems on the theme just mentioned translated by Harekrushna Das are being published in the form of a book. I earnestly hope that this book will provide readers, poets and lovers of literature with emotional and intellectual delight.......

Translator's Note

The poems of Lingaraj Rath offer an insight into the multidimensional workings of a poet's complex imagination. His poems exhibit a range surprisingly wide as the globe itself. The themes the poet dwells upon are revelations of different facets of a poet's personality. The poet is extremely laconic in his expression, but the terseness encapsulates the vision of the whole world. Most of his poems present the poet as an empathetic and sensitive human being who can feel the pain of a wounded bird, and rejoice in the divine manifestation of eternal joy in the objects of Nature. Deeply emotive with the use of carefully chosen words, Rath's poems flow lucidly and rhythmically. They surprise the readers with the impact they create within their compact design that is almost similar to the Haikus.

The present poetry collection is unique of its kind in so far as it consists of poems devoted entirely to the theme of ' poet and poetry. 'Poems of Mr Rath in the original Odia language have been extremely popular among readers and critics owing to their lyrical grace, and the vision and philosophical inclination of the poet. The English rendering of the poems will surely be able to fascinate the readers, and fill their hearts with thrill and joy.

Content

I am a Poet

Give me all the tears of the world
I'll swallow as if 'twere nectar,
Give me all the sorrows of the world
I'll embrace it with a cheer.
I'm a dreamer of all dreams,
   A bard of life's hymns,
'A Poet' is my identity,
I'm portrait of all humanity.

He Alone Can Become a Poet

Tears pushed down throat
Yet always bears a smile,
Never halts on his way
Not even for a while,
Even though lives
In poverty forever,
Walks with majesty
Like an emperor,
Conquers a war
Even without a dagger:
He alone can truly become
A poet in this sphere.

Dream and Struggle

Until tears have been
    Wiped away from eyes,
Until hunger also has been
    Dispelled from stomachs,
Or human child has been
    Unshackled from
    Fetters of cursed night:
My rebellion is undying,
As the dream and struggle of a poet
Is never ever dying.

A Poet's Dream

Would such a day come
When all disputes and enmity
Would vanish beside humanity,
The poet would sing
          victory of verse
Close eyes with delight,
And behold world's beauty.

I'm Therefore A Poet

Sufferings that cannot touch you
Raise storms in my heart,
I always tell those tales
That your lips could not,
I'm therefore a poet:
Ignoring my own anguish
I feel pain of the world.

Poet

Never withers, nor can ever wither
The hopes a poet nurtures,
Never chokes, nor can be choked
The words a poet utters,
Who can smother the voice
      of the never-relenting poet,
Flowing from the lap of hills
It's an ever murmuring rivulet.

Bring Me A Poem

Cheerless sat my sweetheart
Lost in her thought,
Saddened by her wistful looks
Sighed my loving heart,
Asked her if pearls or gems
Could ever bring smiles,
"Pearls are of no use to me,
Bring me a poem ", was her reply.

A Poet Was He

Pained by the lies of the world
Brooding sat he alone,
Pangs of the poor pierced his heart
Tears also drizzled down.
Who's this soul shedding tears
For reasons his were not,
I learnt 'twas no ordinary soul
He's none other than a poet.

Vision of a Poet

Whole creation for a poet
Is benevolent forever,
All creation reveals to him
Omnipresence of creator.

Fearless as always -.
Truth is his only wealth
Dreams are his treasure.

Poet and God

A poet may not be the Omnipotent God
But all he does is creation,
Be it human or mundane creatures
To love all is his religion,
Hatred kills man in the name of God
Rancour destroys the earth,
But a poet's heart is ever ablaze
With love always inflamed his hearth.

More a Sun than a Poet

Sitting in the heart of darkness,
He paints the face of a new morning,
Amid million stars of the night's sky
He keeps his lamps ever glowing,
More a Sun than a Poet is he -
Burning his soul like the wick of a lamp
He dies but illumines everything.

And So I Wrote Poetry

Whole world, even tiny particles-
All filled with mystery...
Wonder-struck and overwhelmed...
I began composing poetry.

Thoroughly a Poet

Who else can melt in grief
At the sorrow of the lonely crane?
Pained at torments and pangs of the world
Shed tears in compassion?

Who else can show up his bosom
And brave the assassin's bullet?
Even if he remains unknown to the world
He is to the core thoroughly a poet.

A Poet

I am not the doom, nor bonfire
I'm not the destroyer-storm:
I'm not untruth, nor a cyclone
Nor a bud nipped before blossom;
A tender soul, I'm a poet -
Never the cause of anyone's sorrow
Never the cause of a gloom.

Never Halts In His Devotion

A Poet always lives his life
In ways grand and imperial,
May he get joy or sorrow
Everything seems him equal,
He may lose as he often gains
Garlands may conceal pricking pains,
Embracing all keeps moving
He sings for God all hymns,
He cares not ever
  applause or censure-
For nothing he halts in his devotion.

Unique Soul

Peacock of his fancy dances gleefully
Even without clouds in the sky,
Deer of his dreams frolics in joy
Fearlessly raising head high,
He knows making nectar off poison
Because he is a poet, uniquely a human.

I Became a Poet

The day you, Oh dear!
Drew my portrait in your heart-
I was born as a poet.

The Poet Struggles

Making his words
        sharp weaponry
The poet struggles a lot,
Oftentimes savours
        the taste of victory
Sometimes he succumbs
        to a defeat.

Do You Know

Do you know
How much of grief
Smoulders in a poet's bosom?
How he sails on
In ocean of life
Gulping down tears of his own?
Keeps on smiling and
Goes on still singing
Life's pious victorious paean,
Searches ever for
The truth of life
Whatever might be his condition.

An Eternal Light

A poet is not a politician
Nor minister or the president,
He spends all his time
Leading human society
Along the virtuous path,
Poetry is where he is bent,
But it is not mere poetry-
Dispelling the dismal
Darkness of life
It is an eternal light.

Destiny of a Poet

Could ever a poet
Tell in his poems
Tender feelings of his heart?
Could ever he express
All he wanted
Touching borders of infinity?
Always remains
Absorbed in his task
Giving form to the formless,
Insatiableness is his destiny
Forever it seems.

Poet's Look

Poetry radiates from his looks
His words murmur as a lyric,
Burns out in darkness
Of our times
Making himself a wick,
An oyster- he makes precious pearls,
His image remains
Untarnished forever
In today's dismal times.

He is Only a Poet

Triumphs in the end
Despite all defeats,
His words always resonate
Even when he is silent,
He is a donor
Even without giving,
He is a rich man
Without a pie or a shilling,
He only is a poet-
A portrait of love ever shining.

Poetry

Poetry flows out
Without cessation
In the breath of a poet,
Poetry is his food and drink
Shelter and his hut.

New Consciousness

A poet can never kill anyone
He is a cause for salvation,
Sanjeevani is the divine knowledge
That a poet alone does own,
Transforms 'thoughts' into 'objects'
Also 'objects' into 'thoughts',
Beacon light of new consciousness
He is armed with bow of creation.

Message of Poetry

Poetry sends out a note:
A new world slowly evolves
While poet is its architect.
A poet pens down lyrics
Portrays consciousness
Of the society
And picture of our times,
Connects diverse spheres of the world
Be it human or non-human lot,
Always spreads message of love
And sings a peaceful note.

Because He's a Poet

A poet brings down
Pious River Ganga
From heaven upon this earth,
Creates beauty of Parijat flowers
Even in gardens of the earth,
Unearths easily many a mystery
Untangles many a knot,
Impossibles are possible for him
Because he is a poet.

A Poet Can Invoke

He can invoke
Rains with his hymns
Even in the heart of a desert,
Amidst scaring darkness of the world
Rays of light is his quest,
Sails on a vessel filled with hopes
Even in the ocean of despair,
Remains composed
With smiles on lips, and
Crosses over to the other shore.
Do you know his identity?
He can be none but a poet.

Breath of a Poet

Poetry flows out incessantly
In the breath of a poet,
Poetry is his food and drink
It is his ultimate rest.

Poet Feels...

A poet is truly queer...
Portrait of the world
Is his bliss,
Always thinks of
Mortals and the Divine
Living and everything lifeless,
A poet is the one that feels,
He can tread even those regions
Where sun cannot find a place.

A Poet Passed Away

A poet passed away
When his life
Ran its destined course,
More salvaged
Than he was dead-
Such was neighbours' solace,
But kith and kins
Moaned in grief
Smouldering in the anguish.
Poetry consoles 'Listen my friends!
A poet never can die,
He is not there
With mortal body
But alive for ages infinite.

If a Poet Wishes...

If a poet wishes...
Fragrance of jasmine
Enthralls all seasons
Cool vernal breeze blows,
All seasons
Sweet fruits may appear,
Drizzles of rain
Any time may shower,
Cuckoo at any time enchants-
If only a poet wishes.

'Poet' Is My Identity

Worshipper of art I am
But black is not my art,
All I pen down is surely truth
But the medium I use is untruth,
My identity is 'a poet',
I am the father
Of vine of poetry
The whole world is my estate.

He Is a Poet

I'd never revealed my heart
But the poet deciphered,
Then he conceived such tales
That I'd never imagined,
Looks and lips, tears and smiles
All are clues to his art,
You can proclaim
To the whole world that
He is none but a poet.

You Are a Poet

You alone can
Adorn the tears
With smiles on lips,
You can drape
The sighs of the heart
With the garb of a bliss.
You're purely a poet, and
Merchant of only feelings,
Drawing portraits of life
You paint even the formless.

Poetry Flows

Poetry flows when
Armour wounds
Crane-couple amorous,
Poetry flows when
In the battleground
Mind of warrior bothers,
Poetry flows when
Mortal-beloved
Love of Kanhu craves,
Poetry flows when
The poet desires
In joy or sorrows
Of divine scheme of cosmos.

Salutes to You

The poet was moving despondent
When a wealthy man enquired:
Sitting atop heaps of wealth
I cannot ever find peace,
But when I read a poem of yours
I feel entrenched in bliss,
You always shower upon me
Whatever I wish,
Salutes therefore to you O poet
Salutes for your artifice.

You Call Me a Poet

You call me a poet
But I am a sentinel,
Absorbed in my duty
I never bother for trifle.
I keep composing poems
All through day and night,
And safeguard the humanity
From the stinking plight.
Write-ups with putrid thoughts
Are nothing but only poison,
For wellbeing of the human world
I lash at such nuisance.

I lead all thoughts and feelings
Along the virtuous path,
A sentinel of society
I am known upon this earth.

Poetry Is Life

A poet is lost
The whole night
In the melancholy
Ocean of poetry,
His days are
Sometimes joyous
In the grace of poetry,
Poetry is his life-
All his bliss
In such a life,
Many a time
He takes such birth.

Second Creator.

Absorbed forever
In creative thoughts,
Defies challenges
That obstruct his paths,
Meditation is his affair-
A poet is the second creator.

Poetry Claims

Human beings seek self-interest
Appease their mean desires,
Poetry seeks to fight against
Injustice forever,
Always nurturing uncommon thoughts
Builds a new world with care.

Messenger of Peace

Poet sings for
The victory of poetry,
The victory of power
Is all humans celebrate,
But what comes out in the end?
Lust for power causes bloodshed,
Poetry is the messenger of peace
Peace ultimately triumphs.

I Live in Poetry

I'm a poet, I live in poetry,
Poetry is my breath;
It's my shelter, and my life
Here will I meet my death.

I Can See the Unseen

Agony that shatters
the bosom of the distressed
Causes tremors in my heart;
Suffering that ravages
the life of the oppressed
Smothers my sighing throat;
I can fathom pains, pangs, and
Immense depth of oceans;
I can discern desperate yearnings
Of bleak minds and their concerns;
I can see the unseen;
Always tread untrodden paths
I'm therefore a Poet.

I Tread along Untrodden Paths

I tread along untrodden paths
And reveal the heart of facts
Evil ways, words, company and thoughts
Are to me far and distant.
Never halt on my journey-
Care not I for praise or censure
Because I am a poet.

I Seek

Scorching heat of summer seeks
Soothing showers of rain,
Mind chilled in deadly winter
Seeks cool breeze of the spring,
But I seek, O Poetry, all the seasons
Silent shelter of your bosom
And your smiles enchanting.

Garland of Grief Girdles

Garland of grief girdles him
Still smiles dazzle on his lips,.
Never considers fires of danger
Hurdles on his paths,
Sings ballads of tears
Upon lyre of life,
'I'm after all a poet '
He exults with such identity.

My Greatest gift

I am a poet who forever suffers
Rejection and neglect,
Never wish for the emperor's throne
Money or any present,
Accept my humble request:
Feel the heart of my poems,
That will be my greatest gift.

Identity of a Poet

Who knows a poet,
What is his capacity?
Poetry is his only passion
And his lone identity.
Nurtures tender dreams
Only to become a poet,
Wealth,honours and awards
Are never its equal slot.
Give him if you can
A little love and respect,
It is nectar for him
To conquer even death.

Poet Comes

Ruthless summer
Often singes
Whole world with heat,
Season of spring
Builds up a rainbow
In the mind and heart.
When the rains
Pour out
Nectar bowl of bliss,
Mind exults
With touch of
Autumn silver beams

When the untold miseries
Die in the heart,.
Tears of grief
Like a fountain
Flows out,
Then with a poem in hand
Humbly comes a poet.

For Which I'm a Poet.

I painted a lot of portraits of yours
Not a one could please me.
Your charming form flashed upon
Mirror of my heart in solitude.
What a marvellous portrait!
More a poem than mere portrait
For which I'm today a poet.

I'm Ever Defiant

My heart cares not for
Hurdles or doubts,
My work never cares for
Tiredness or shouts,
My feet never pause
For want of rest,
For fear of enemies
My hands never retreat-
For I'm a poet
An ever-defiant portrait.

I Don't Know How

I picked up the brush
To paint your portrait,
I do not know how
I turned an artist.

I was looking for a tune
To sing hymns in your praise,
I am still not aware how
I turned a singing bard.

I had picked up my pen
To narrate your virtues,
I wonder forever how
I was transformed into a poet.

Thinking Only Of Poetry

Never do I want
Awards or honours
Pearls, gems or diamonds,
Just wish
To bathe in poetry
Falling in love with poems.
Dispel from mind all fears-
Turning toward
The haven of poetry
Enjoy the bliss of its juice.

Who Can Be His Match

No one has ever seen
Flowers of the heaven,
But a poet alone plucks
Such dream flowers
Falling in their love.
He swims across the fog, and
Causes Time to pause...
A unique human being he is
Who can ever be his match?

Because I'm a Poet

Flames of tear
Couldn't burn me out
Torments have
Hardened me a lot,
Upon the ocean of despair
Hopes always sail my boat,
I survive
In this world of sorrows
Because I am a poet.

He's Called a Poet

Weapon of laughter in his hand,
Brave fighter in this world,
Life for whom is sheer meditation,
Service of truth his only devotion,
Lives his life
Tears gulped down the throat,
He alone is fit
To be addressed a poet.

In Love with Poetry

I am poetry and not a damsel
Different from others,
Damsel peeves but poetry smiles
Never brings doleful tears,
Heart often bleeds and wounds
Even though
You may surrender it to lasses,
Fall in love with poetry and see-
It will fight with your sorrows.

I'm There for You

Why worry if ever you see
Morbid moon in the grey skies,
Why look so sad O Spring
Because gone are your days,
Never worry, Oh never worry:
I am there for you, a poet,
I am with you in your sorrows
Giving off hands of support.

Poetry Is Mightier

Desires never know extinction
Sorrows do not know an end,
Pen of a poet is still mightier
Poetry is greater a command.

A Poet Never Dies

Humans meet their end
        Plants wither away
                Brimming river also dries,
Spring disappears
        Monsoon fades away
                But a poet never dies.

Not Easy To Be Poet.

If you don't sink
In the ocean of hope-
You cannot become a poet,
If you don't burn
In the flames of emotion-
You cannot become a poet,
If you don't move along
The path of equality-
You cannot become a poet,
If you don't give up
All hypocrisy and treachery-
You cannot become a poet.

Absorbed In His Work

The world smiles
With the smile of a poet
Foliage smiles upon the forest,
Sighs and tears of the poet
Rends bosom of the earth,
A poet is truly a monk-
Gathers fondly all in his embrace
He is absorbed in his work.

Life   of A Poet

A poet wakes up with poetry,
Spends day in such thought,
Afternoons inch away
In lap of poetry
As he engages in a chat,
Poetry sings lullabies for him
As he goes to sleep at night.

The World Calls Me a Poet

I give words to the inexpressible
Render form to the formless,
Reflecting all that's unthinkable
Mould with creative traces,
The world calls me a poet,
In the world of falsity and lies
I paint only portraits of truth.

His Life Is Spent

A poet is worldly, often ascetic
He is also a rebel,
Also appears in this world
In a reformer's role.
He is universally known,
Spends life like Prajapati- the creator
Always shaping his creation.

Poet: A Warrior Celestial

A poet is a warrior celestial,
The one whom he kills
With the arrow of his poetry
Surely becomes immortal.

A poet may someday pass away
His days come to a closure,
But the one whose bosom
Has embraced the poet's arrow
Remains alive forever.

Destined Lot

A poet may grow old
But his poetry forever young-
It is the destined lot.

Poet since Birth

Poetry is quite dearer to me
Than is my soul,
Poetry loves me intensely
Than does my damsel,
Poetry flows all over my being
Even through my breath,
I therefore could become
A poet since my birth.

I'm Thoroughly a Poet

I am thoroughly a worldly fellow
Also a great ascetic,
Embrace the whole world as my own
Never turn choleric.
I keep painting its portrait-
All are very dear to my heart
I am thoroughly a poet.

Who Really Knows a Poet

He's never been saddled
                  on the throne of pelf
Never lost in the game
                  of interest of his self.
Does he ever wield
                  the weapons of power?
Mad for love, affection-
                  He's a human being so poor.
He is only a poet-
But who really knows a poet?

Sad Song of My Heart

This is not dry, barren poetry
But sad song of my heart,
These tears are not mere drops of water
They reveal tales of my heart,
I reel at a deep thought,
Flaming my own funeral pyre
With sorrows, I burn out.

Desires of A Poet

I haven't got anything in life
Still achieved a lot,
I am emperor of my world
Never care for others' thought.
I have sung the psalms of life
Judging life and truth,
I bow my head to Almighty
Thinking welfare of the world.

Do Not Consider Me Alien

I am a paean of your delight
Also a sigh lying in your heart,
A member of your family
I speak of your joy and plight,
Do not consider me an alien lot,
I am a poet, a humane poet.

Tenets of a Poet

New moon night turns moon blanched
In the words of a poet,
Darkness is dispelled from mind
Fears gone from the heart,
Poet keeps on singing forever
Undying songs of hope,
Beams of light, full of delight-
Tenets of a poet's life.

All Are My Friends

Moon is my companion
Along with all stars,
Spring often leans down
To have with me chatters,
Monsoon comes in sullen face
To share with me her grief,
Tears of sorrow and heartbreak
Flow down making her sick,
Flowers and birds enchant me
As allure oceans and forests,
I feel bliss in their laps
As spend my days and take rest,
A poet, I will keep singing
Songs of joy for everyone,
All are very dear to me
All are my companion.

Life Of A Poet

I've suffered since I became a poet
But no one knows my pain,
I've sung many songs of grief
But none has heard such strain,
Became happy and danced with joy
But no one has seen my delight,
These are memories in a poet's life-
But no thought given by a wight.

King and Poet

King and poet travelled together
Beyond bounds of their state,
The poet was acclaimed in that land
But the king remained a stranger-guest.

I Keep Going

A poet, I have composed poetry
On tales of the timid Partha,
Exposed love stories about
Unholy amorous act,
Enjoyment now looms large
In the guise of sacrifice,
The world labeled me insane
When I portrayed all profligacy.
I keep going on my path-
I wish I could ever achieve
The destination I want!

A Poet Spends His Time

Spring sends letters
Through the poet
To the Queen Earth,
Northern cool winds
Come when the poet
Carries the Winter's heart,
Honeybee sends
Message to the flower
Making poet his messenger,
Carrying the moon's
Letter to the Lily
The poet spends his hours.

I Sing Of Humanity

A poet I never bother to know
If you are a poor or rich man,
Never do I care whether you are
A Hindu or a Musselman,
I do not wonder about one's caste
Never harbour such thought,
Which country one inhabits
I time and again forget.
All are humans - I consider,
Singing ever of humanity
I find nectar everywhere.

A Poet Swings

Nights of a poet
Trudge before the daybreak,
Lest sweet dreams
Of the poor man should break,
Morning's always reluctant
To set in so soon,
The poet always swings
In the lap of imagination.

Don't You Ever Know

A poet is always forgetful
Of his domestic chores,
For which once with his wife
He fell into bitter bickers,
He was sitting dumbfounded
Lost in despondency,
Poetry whispered in his ears
'Give me all your worries;
She is only your wife
This is what people know,
But I am your real beloved-
Don't you ever know?'

Time Is My Judge

A poet, I write never wish for
Applause or garlands of flower,
I give shape to all the thought
That crowd up in the heart.
I nourish a craving forever for
Truth, Beauty and Godliness,
I tread along only those paths
That my conscience allows.
Time is my greatest judge:
Transient praise or criticism
What after all is their use?

I Sing of a New Era

All rituals and stereotypes
      That prevail in the society-
A poet, I have freed myself
      From fetters of those laws,
I sing of a new epoch
      Rejecting all superstitions
May people's conscience rise
      And world smile with cheers.

Current of Peace

Ministers and courtiers
Of a state sat thoughtful,
Defence of the enemy attack
Made everyone fretful,
Witless and clueless
They sought solace from the king,
But unfazed king just smiled
Without even worrying,
'Send a noble poet to that land '
Said the king with ease,
'He can silence all violence
And create current of peace. '

I Want to Know

Cannot you ever see O Lord
The world you have created?
How does life move on, of the
Downtrodden and the tortured?
Tears flood in the eyes of widow
Orphans breathe sigh and fear,
Untold torments suffer the poor
Longing death in despair.
Tell this poet O Creator!
Do you really love to see
Eyes blind with tear?

I Weigh Vice and Virtue

I weigh all vice and virtue
I am a fearless poet,
I will surely show to the world
What is its true portrait.

Virtuous here often
      Considered a sinner,
Sinner is gifted with
      Heaven and nectar,
I am witness to the
      Hide and seek of
      All vice and virtue,
I will go in search of the truth.

Poetry Vibrates With Life

Poetry is a fountain of thought
Flowing down from the heaven,
Ocean of pure enlightenment
Haven of pearls and gems,
Poetry radiates joy and solace-
Source of bliss and peace,
Poetry vibrates with life
Ineffable, and endless.

My Meditation with Words

Sporting with my armory of words
I display all my skills,
More sense is hidden underneath
Than as much is revealed,
Those words often reveal
In my mind
Myriad novel forms,
I am enchanted and delighted:
I meditate with words.

The Greatest Poet

The world sparkles
        With your creation
        Gentle divine songs,
Forests, rivers, meadows
        Even mountains
        All bear your imprints,
Planets and stars...
        This vast universe
        How magnificently conceived!
A poet I am ever mesmerized
To witness the splendid poetry.
You are the greatest poet,
Bless me O Lord!
My life may sail on
Only with your thought.

A Poet's Mission

A poet, I move in my mission
The grand road in my front,
I am not sure whether I will win
Or I will fall to the ground,
'Words' is my peer armour
'Feelings' is my shield,
Caring not for any hurdle
I march with my play of words.

Poetry Flows

I am a poet and never a Maoist
Still my blood curdles,
Whenever the world puts
Shackles of slavery
In the hands of innocents,
When a destitute
Wails in distress
Sans food and shelter,
Rebellious thoughts
Stir up in mind
And makes my heart sore:
My pen cannot
Remain silent
Poetry flows like a river.

Poet's Appeal

Grant my meager wish O Lord
I do not want any salvation,
Until the day, I breathe my last
Fill my heart with your devotion.
May I never harm anyone
Even if I cannot extend help,
Never may I slander anyone
Grant this wish for my sake.
This is all that this poet wants:
Bless me that
I never bow my head
Never stretch begging hands.

The Poet Awakens

Pained by the grief
Of the conjugating cranes,
You have sung O Poet
 The history of the Mahabharata tales.
The ways you have shown through
Epics and many poems,
Everything is flung to air
In the decadent storms.
Culture and civil ways
All values are lost,
Floods of degeneration
Drown today's world.
The poet therefore awakens...
To protect our values that are
Eternal and ageless.

Won't Write Poetry

A poet I swear
I will not ever more
Pen down any poem,
What use of writing if
No one grasps the sense?
I do not know caste or nation
Nor have I any religion,
I am always absorbed
Dreaming welfare of man.
I have sung in many poems
Psalms of truth and peace,
But I am rent by the
Ravage of violence.
Discontent reigns
To watch this spectacle
Even after writing many poems,
Therefore I swear
I will never ever
Pen down more poems.

Tired of Writing Poetry

Tired of writing poetry whole life
I feel spiritless to write more,
Sickened by witnessing the world
I feel pained to watch more,
My eyelids droop in misery-
I will therefore travel much far
Thinking only of poetry.

Poetry: My Pilgrimage

A poet, I keep writing poetry...
Writing is my religion,
Whatever be the vocation
Writing is my obsession,
I sing the triumph of
" Satya- Shiva- Sundara "
And portray it in poetry
Being humble and sincere,
My devotion is dedicated
At the feet of poetry,
Poetry is my religion
My whole life until death.

Poet Is Mirthful

Diction of a poet
Is the carol of bird
He smiles like a child,
His eyes brim with
Pity, compassion,
Optimism and trust,
Poet is full of mirth,
He treads the path
Of peace and truth-
Destroying all untruth.

Then The Poet Writes

When flowers of dream
Wither away, and
Heart breaks into pieces,
Spring of hopes
Vanish in summer, and
Garden of heart wrecks-
The poet composes poems,
Nectar rains through the poetry
All that is lost is regained.

Black Eagle Books

www.blackeaglebooks.org
info@blackeaglebooks.org

Black Eagle Books, an independent publisher, was founded
as a nonprofit organization in April, 2019. It is our mission
to connect and engage the Indian diaspora and the world at
large with the best of works of world literature published on
a collaborative platform, with special emphasis on
foregrounding Contemporary Classics and New Writing.